I0815162

As Long as We're Here

Also by Joel Brouwer

Exactly What Happened

Centuries

And So

Off Message

As Long as We're Here

Poems

Joel Brouwer

Library of Congress Cataloging-in-Publication Data

Names: Brouwer, Joel, 1968- author
Title: As long as we're here : poems / Joel Brouwer.
Other titles: As long as we are here
Description: New York : Four Way Books, 2026.
Identifiers: LCCN 2025027263 (print) | LCCN 2025027264 (ebook) | ISBN 9781961897786 trade paperback | ISBN 9781961897793 ebook
Subjects: LCGFT: Poetry
Classification: LCC PS3552.R68245 A93 2026 (print) | LCC PS3552.R68245 (ebook) | DDC 811/.54--dc23/eng/20250626
LC record available at https://lccn.loc.gov/2025027263
LC ebook record available at https://lccn.loc.gov/2025027264

This book is manufactured in the United States of America and printed on acid-free paper.

Four Way Books is a not-for-profit literary press. We are grateful for the assistance we receive from individual donors, public arts agencies, and private foundations including the New York State Council on the Arts, a state agency.

We are a proud member of the Community of Literary Magazines and Presses.

Contents

The stars are putting on their glittering belts.
They throw around their shoulders cloaks that flash
Like a great shadow's last embellishment.

—Wallace Stevens, "The Auroras of Autumn"

An Onset of Palsy

We insisted excitement be always near to hand
and reliable industries arose. In the mid-eighteenth century
the postal service in England had yet to achieve
this measure of trust. In ours, after morning threw
its silver over the oily horizon, we were insatiable
and chill by turns all day, tracking packages
out for delivery, then opening our breathing apps.
Planes scraped chalk across the green summer sky.
Some real trees were harvested while others
just fell to their knees like toddlers in a tantrum.

Or something low-poly like that. Exaggeration
being pretty much impossible. Everyone
in the chat acts amazed by disappointment
as if it isn't the rule. I recommend folks slow down
and focus their thoughts, picture them as parcels
ascending a gentle conveyor and vanishing

one by one into a certain smuggled gloom.
We should expect our failed familiars to desert us
after so much silence, or maybe deference
has strangled them like a girl winding a lank tendril
of hair tight around her finger, or lianas
deleting a jungle temple from the sat map.

The ancient fires yet smolder. The great apes
fear rivers. Further efforts to engender pleasure
or surprise gradually unravel over the course
of the work week. Seen from above on the webcam
my father's sleeping body occupies the corner
of his mattress like an envelope's return address.

Velleities of May

Assured their deaths were in effect a cure
for what ailed them, they said sure whatever
and signed their names and did unto others.
Or tried to. I'll start pouring, you say when.
You can't imagine how many trumpets
thereafter mustered in the forecourt. I admired us
for taking it on. High command vanished
along with the chattering classes, unwilling
or unable to trace a full arc while hoppers
of rotting grain pouted on the sidings.
We none of us expected justice from mice.
Everyone got the memo. Those nearest
shore gathered their thoughts and gave voice
to else statements and faint sprites
we only later understood to be both logical
and a heck of a lot less egalitarian than

anyone knew. People joke about manure.
There's nothing funny about it. And it wasn't
so much what we feared as it was a means
of keeping water from flooding the ocean
and the desert from burning the sand.
Yes, we had near misses, but Rick's bully boys
and a bit of baksheesh got us over the hump.
Predictable crimes chewed up the dreamy glow
adrift among twilight's traffic lights like—
well, like apricot mist if I can say it like that—
while we, the pie makers, the sober souls
who gave early and often, caught all the hell
despite what some strangers recalled. Them
again. The strivers, the whiz kids. Rick said
checking into the clinic a few days late
gave him a real shot in the arm. Ha ha.

But I'm not going to lie, they knuckled down
and literally planted a flag. So badass
and frosty out there—at least at first blush.

1000 Hours of Staring

We fucked around, found out, and what do you know?
Upside patterns blossomed everywhere.
And it ain't over yet! Insiders ignore the trash talk
while we, to maintain appearances, pass our days
holed up in a MoMA restroom, holding our breath
to avoid registering an aesthetic opinion
(and detection). If winter loosens and leaks
across the page like spilled white ink, the critics
will say we wasted our chance. To feel it, I mean.

It's unlikely any season will come again. Discernment
having slipped into a sort of corporation, smooth
as something unbelievably smooth, locked
in spheres, partisan as a mutton-headed mugwump
despite the clinically proven benefits
of both variance and small heaps of sand spread
across the prairie, speaking for themselves, as far

as you can see. A spirit tilts the vents.

I circulate. I mutate. I'm a virus but I'm cute.

College Days

Yes, the whole enchilada was planned
in advance, including Barrett
doing a handstand in the library.
Now he says he can't commit. The four
categories I put my feelings in
were days, weeks, months, and years.
Can we go back to your place and see
what there is to eat? Susan walked
as a giant might. We assumed a citizen
journalist recorded it. It was a summer night
but it wasn't a joyful summer night
and before long I'd developed spasms
of the intestines. Even a little bug
is filled with incredible textures.
If you ask me, those people have every right
to come over here, present
their questions, and take all the time

they need. The space between

stars is scary. We have to live with that.

Screenshot

She said in a very real sense
letting go and holding on

can't be distinguished in the dark.
The fact that certain words

were chosen with all due diligence
doesn't mean others couldn't

have worked just as good.
You learn a lot at a drag strip!

My final wisps of faith
are history, and sorry not sorry

I knew it was coming when
grown-ass adults gathered at dusk

in the cul-de-sac to break down
cardboard boxes. I was late

to call bullshit, and over the next
few years, despite rising seas

and lowkey productive
peace talks, we mostly stayed

put, while others were just
getting started, bouncing around

every which way but up. No harm
no foul. She said to hold on

and loaned me most of her logins.
The peculiar tones and contours

of my loneliness failed to find
an audience, so we planned to return

the rental car and stick to the original
intention of settling down

with a conservative interpretation
of the fourth movement

to feature, you guessed it, clarinet.
That oughta fry some bacon.

She said take your trouble over there.
Then she herself went over there.

To keep my trouble company?
This was specifically in the TV room

which always felt so fancy to us.
A genuine popcorn machine!

Uncle Chip kept a stoic octopus
under a purple lamp

and puffed on Kools. At home
we may have lacked commodities

but we were dumb enough
to understand radical individualism

was a movement doomed
to be boring forever and ever.

Men came to repossess the sofas
shortly after that. I for one

appreciated the clarity. Come back
in a week or so, once you've made

better friends. Suction offers a similar
pleasure, and it's no wonder

so many pick it up in the course
of their studies. She said

can you take two steps to the left
to block my view

of the moon, I've seen more
than enough of her lately, I suppose

she'd say the same of me, stuff
like that. About a half dozen bats

wheeled above the streetlight
which seemed to track

given the context, but at the last
second, I remembered

just because you can imagine something
that doesn't make it true.

Like no matter how old a book gets
it'll never be a good listener.

I was glad our former teachers
weren't around to see us chewing

on that. She had tools you could
use, but only in a dream, when really

it's a challenge we need to address
as a planet. Sucks to be you.

Let's skip the full soup and fish
and see if we can get away

with feathers and a fake ID.
Some of the least politic among us

might still identify, or even
overcome adversity, and I want you

to meet Ariel's group before they
get too tired to invent

more trouble for us. Yes, seriously.
Why would I butter you up

when this dump is literally hiring

randos off the street?

She said from now on she wanted

her nickname to be "Smiley"

and we had to explain it's not

like the before times, you don't choose

your own nickname, burglars

break in to give you things, nurses

saunter along the corridors, a few

eggs last a month. Most animals

will admit they don't know

what they don't know, and that's how

you steer clear of the rocks. She said
OK sue me, but it boils down to

one bad decision in the river. So smug
we had evaded the curse

we had coming, when it would have been
better to lie down and take it

hot and dirty, after the malady's aspects
had slowed to a stop. You'll have

that dang baby, I know it in my bones.
I saw it following protocol

in the screenshot, and autumn
has admitted everything, and even if we turn

back on the tarmac as the mist
rolls in, even if we try sticking it

in rice, it's still dead easy to forget
how cringe the evening's been.

If I Recall Correctly

Picture please a brace of heroes from the past
seeming at first to ignore us but at the last moment
lending their faces, ablaze with capacity.
Our cherished fears vanquished with a puff of steam.
Our bums in the butter. Rude youths forded
the river wearing everyday attire. I declined to sign
the loyalty oath for obvious reasons.

Some of the catch-farts greeted the new normal
by wiping hard drives long past dark. The monsignor
called for his burn barrel to be brought
into the chapel. I think the late wars had cemented
or perhaps I should say captured
an itch for ignorance which the heroes
dialed in on and conveyed with a caress.

These punishments are maybe too mushy. If I sound
unreasonable I'm lying on the marble floor in the nave
trying to do everyone's living for them
and working up rough plans for dying.
Lying or laying. I was told none of the straights
would pipe down during lights-out quiet hour.
There's always fresh adult jetsam to be ignored.

A blue aperture stops down as dusk rises
in the valley, pinches to black, in effect surrenders.
The nights stand firm, and we resist.
I've never been what you'd call sprightly
but I've had purpose as well as something a lot like it.
If I recall correctly, a great calm purred up
through the blood then, soft and under construction.

Girl with Gazelle

She vaults the fence like a proof of concept
and we surrender to her joy. For once
we're in the clear, sky-high, as spring's minty
fingers press color through the canvas.
I feel like I'm doing all the talking. Out back
friends struck the tent, since we'd agreed
that area wanted to be vacant. It's mostly clay.
You were discreet, but I knew you had a bunch
of sentences ready to deploy—whether
kudos, judgments, observations, or whatever
I had no clue. The sublime dissolves upon
its apprehension. Maybe that area wanted
to be a rookery? If these structures
become normalized, then any garden jumble
stands to garner just as much respect
as the finest high street shops, thus proving
my point. I've long been blind to the flies

who would woo the devil with their sparkle

and hunches. So, individually, we're safe.

My cousin discovered this painting in his garage.

I think it's wanting me to sit with it a spell.

Letting go of the illusion that my thoughts

interest others has honestly made

them much more exciting to me. My heart

is in my pocket, it is an unboxing video

reacting to vintage naughty ephemera. I mean

as long as we're here don't mind if I do.

Wrapped in Black and Yellow

By the time you read this, cooler heads will surely
have prevailed, so I expect the countdown
can continue. The atoms failed to carom. The new fabric
of national communion is woven
largely from threads that had made up other fabrics.
But listen, before all that, let's round up
a group of people who haven't died yet and see
what they think. I didn't enjoy my fitting, no.
They didn't follow basic business etiquette
and apparently their Airbnb in Albuquerque
was a teepee? There's plenty of beer here.
The consensus is you can count on me.

When the kids come back, we must be blunt.
Early on we forfeited the benefits of dying
at home, and unlike the others we stuck
to the plan, separating the dancer

from the dance in the same grand tapestry
sunrise pledges and withholds. Priests in our parish
are reliving the past and its sadness
despite the warm bronze earth beneath their feet.
Given how little these weak sticks wrapped
in black and yellow seem to trouble anyone
why bother prosecuting? There's a club downtown
with apathetic acts I think you'll love.

It's Been a Real Rollercoaster

So profound was our poverty the crickets

would not sing for us, and in order to converse

with other dreamers we were obliged to use

web-based translation engines. My jewels

mere paste, of course. You knew it full well

but were too sweet, or too small, to say. You can

tell this next one's a waltz because of the way

that it is. Other things that won't help at all

include an afternoon on the tarmac socked in

by snow, back-of-the-envelope shenanigans, and—

though the country club set can't shut up

about it—a literal suit of armor. I made a reckless

error. I believed it was all about the work.

My lover's smock is blue against the universe.

*

When mercurochrome shadows steal over
the agency, we'll signal the hired hands
to sally forth into the brush as planned, targeting
our blasts but keeping the tone nice and light.
A dozen deep breaths should do it. Your whole
laugh-now-cry-later style has flooded the city
like an awful but sexy drug—as if they thought
they had no ponies but they do. Would it make
the proletariat any gentler if we blew up
their spot? Resentment is a bridge to strut
across, fearless in the face of slack skin
and doomscrolling teens, fixed as the words
in a book you once loved and likely as dumb.
That the ocean has a gender makes it worse.

*

No, you're right, I'm plenty intentional
and my singing's okay. I'm the chap who wiped
the final bias from the ol' scoreboard
and bid the children honeyed slumber. No one
grasps apathy is the new black, at least
none of these chumps pounding down the doors
for a peek at my icon collection. Seems
the more finespun my thinking becomes the less
I can get it up to give a hoot, and you can
stamp that on a pancake, hermano. I almost
said "such is our age," and you saw it coming
a mile away, and you granted me a tender nudge
and you smelled like Florida, and you said
the quiet part out loud, but still pretty quiet.

Smash or Pass

Did you notice one of the extras in that hospital scene
kept looking into the camera, as if a clearer future
was coming right at him? Surely by now I've forgotten
more than I know. I coddle my orchids and rewind

my shows. When animals stand still in a sunny pasture
I assume they're thinking of evening. You've never
been one to push a song on anyone, at least that's been
my experience, or to label the system of attachment

that has grown, over these last weeks, as complex
and hot as an anthill. The heap of unprimed canvas
on the studio floor reminds me of a Buddha
in a temple with no roof. Yet I love that you cherish

your weakness and mine. I guess most of the livestock
are happy with grass. Smash or pass. Smash or pass.

Fancy That

We were warned to expect awkward clothes
and poisons, and that any number of angels
would ring us up from hell with tales of woe
once the do-somethings won the election
by shouting listicles down the gullies
of the mainstream media and feigning
affection for horses. Not on my block
it's true—I've had about as much
of the incels as I intend to take—
but above my jacuzzi's sizzle I can hear
the klaxons and their grim command to catalog
the oils and ointments I've enjoyed.
I'm a team player and an open book.
Might I please be loaned the price of a ticket
to Sanary-sur-Mer or some other
problematic place? I've stuffed my ruck
and willed a fiction per request. There can be

no suffering loftier than mine, as the angel
of boredom has undressed herself
for me and cooked a fair soup. Yes, really.
We all saw the news about how mountains
"wince" and how the nacreous mist up there
deadens all sound, especially laughter.
Go ahead, don't believe me. After flowers
rhetoric was the first thing we surrendered.

After Overhearing a Confidential Conversation

I'd planned an exclusive and sentimental dinner
with a few local edgelords after spotting them
dumping salt into the sea, and you'd agreed
to close your eyes. Now we reap what we've sown.
A cheese course colloquy that will. Not. End.
What do tadpoles and caterpillars have in common?
No, besides that. Correctamundo: A noble silence.
Henceforth the burnt earth shall reflect
our half-felt convictions, and the tarry skid
shall veer over the embankment exactly as
expected. We deny what we denied. My opinion
of the current administration is useless
as a cloud, but here it is anyway, in triplicate.

Luckily few see much daylight between pathos
and whatever its opposite is. If you happen
to catch that window open, go ahead and check

whether there's a bird out there, and then
hit me back, OK? I'll just be itching my hickeys
and jamming to yacht rock all weekend.
Avoid your fate? Sister, you're soaking in it.
As for memories, though my feeling for them grows
shaggier and sweeter as the present presses
its case onstage, I won't deny an average day
of donuts, excess leverage, a jar full of fireflies
and things of that nature would suit me fine
in lieu of all but the crème de la crème.

Purchasing Power

Close to sober, trending on the network
singing competition "Pit of Fire," it don't make

me no nevermind if a couple flyover
junior senators put me on blast or pump

a vision of their knee-jerk patrimony. I sleep
in a hollow log on a mountainside.

Where it's peaceful! While my only dad
relies on analgesics to spot fakes from the war.

Listen, I felt good in the thick of it, that was
never the issue. I just couldn't connect

with the tea-scented crescendos of chiffon
the empire insisted upon back then.

You're welcome to your pleasure. If we toy
with the ratios, or if the odd man turns out bad

and must take a back seat, so be it.
Bravery's a fable. Cowardice

is a faith. If I could retrieve the ink
I've spilled, and my business card collection, and

perhaps half my unanswered questions, or
even just that last brandy and soda

you'd be free to let me go and call me
a stranger, a gift of gold and spices

sunk in the Moluccas. When we got home
the village was deserted. I saw a wolf

in the cards. Remember how the coach
compulsively clicked his stopwatch

at practices? Like he was carving out
a bit of time to stash our fictions in.

So-Called Vernacular Architecture

The research shows we have more options than ever
which put another way means we must expend more
and more energy rejecting possibilities. To our credit
we can agree the past is a currency in free fall.
Get with it, comrades. It's late in the game and rival gangs
in the mountain towns need thoughtful leadership.
You know I'm dead serious because I pause
at the window to supervise the night sky's sigh
from violet to gray. As I peel a tangerine with feeling.

Who's this dug a burrow in my body? Our teenagers
have fled the countryside in record numbers to savor
quick freedoms in the city, and we can't legislate
away even this gentle despair, this hard flat spark
the infectious among us might at any given moment
extinguish or issue. My friends and I have registered
for a course in practical censorship. I'm alert

to the immediacy of the central tenets and context
clues. But are we too late? Could you rewind

and play me that last part back again? All dazzled, addled
by drought, our late intrigues now seem dull as toast
on a wintry morning, and those who have earned our trust
by keeping mum would as soon keep it that way. A window
painted shut, proud nations defending their lands, clouds
brassy and fixed at twilight. Are you really worse off?
I suppose drunks and shamans may say so and spur zealots
into covertly orchestrated fracases. From here I'm getting
mostly comedy and a stack of buttermilk flapjacks.

Sonnet Found in a Borrowed Book

A shadow so rudely diminished the fresh sculpture
in the boudoir we felt compelled to drag our asses
back out on the hustings and affirm a value or two.
We call it our forfeit pageant. The horses in it

surprise me every time, because horses never lie.
Personally, I'm happy it's harder than ever
for the village harbingers to turn any heads.
Days are deaths, you know that. Our ancestors

plunked us in a bucket, and lately the babies
harmonize like forsaken cicadas, but mercy me.
When ye olde tricks no longer pay the rent
we learn to live with damp kindling and sincerity.

You melt bronze, I crack granite. Then again
I love when you muss me up against an evening.

Brown Study

Word is we're the folks best positioned to speak
whether off the cuff or following brown study
glancing off camera into the dusk beyond
the fresnels, where, frankly, we store our hopes.
They're so tiny you might have missed them

or mistaken them for fears, much as dances
are sometimes called "choreography come to life."
Let's truly focus now. We're all pretty helpless.
The light is changing fast and shadows stain
our congress indigo and tan. If we're going to have

a productive meeting, we need to surprise ourselves
roll up our cuffs and plunge into fresh deeds.
Notice anything new? Not really. Our volunteer crocus
parts its yellow lips among the smoky hyacinths
much like last year and the year before last.

Low and Away

Even our laziest users have long since uninstalled that bird
and soup identification app. The problem tends to be content
or discontent. We're either antiseptic or getting someone

arrested. I try to hang easy. I drift in political fog. I voted
for the lady with the free hot dogs. Probably for me the least helpful
TV series was that one with all those talkative people in it.

O longsuffering tongue, where you at? Together we trucked
reams of trash to hell, merry as cartoon bandits
and sure as shit our souls would effervesce and worm their way

into the past once we had our bars on lock. I'm looking to sell
but the market's dried up. Today's sadness level is medium.
We could take the tram to the harbor for moules-frites

as per usual, rehearse the fables, and count ourselves among
the lucky ones. It might feel better afterwards. Holding out candies
right at eye level, my suitemates made good on their pledge

to delay the inevitable. My dad called in the middle of it
with updated information regarding the chemical processes
occurring in our coffee cups. It seemed best to roll with this.

We were regular people in regular rooms, exchanging remarks.
If we managed to get a few in edgewise when the pond was still pink
let's call it a win. You can build a little hut with the leftover wood.

No Big Mystery

After the farmers left, some of us hung back
to compare notes, and I wondered how long
before my thoughts began to spoil.
It wasn't that anyone had misspoken themselves—
let's just say more than one wagon
had lost its wheels. It got a lot colder
at sunset, and no one felt like grabbing dinner.
Time grew short. The drums got loud.
We were late to condemn the occupation
and assumed high alert and sour rations
were on the horizon. Clearly it would be weird
to refuse, and hole up all August tangled
with our rivals in a ball of smoke while the kids—
junior diplomats—chucked crabapples dipped
in mud at cars prowling down the avenue.

We should keep moving. There's much more
to know. Those who headed for the dim hills
text dire emojis day and night, and I can't
be the only sucker to shoulder it or run my finger
over the latch on the infirmary cabinet.
Almost all the blood you saw in those photos
was 100% authentic. To me, that's a relief.
Breezes and waves I once took for meaningless
now seem like valid questions, questions
that melt into a turquoise sludge when asked aloud.
On n'en finira jamais avec la sensation.
Even refugees holding perfectly still under
the water will make a little noise sometimes
and a few wear earrings. I'd prefer one future
to a bunch of them, at least I think so.

Saturn Return

As you know, the universe is quite large
and our chances of picking out the sound
of any specific singer remain low. Kids

who were once so solicitous no longer pay
any mind. You may suggest we husband
our resentments, but to insist the coup

couldn't have been predicted extends
an already overlong parley disguised
as a French feminism conference in Boise.

You heard me, gramps. I'm calling you in.
Most nights we ran to the sea
to redeem our excess joy, while our brokers

smoked a smidge of hash and built worlds
on their phones. The stark order of sex
disagrees with me. I like to stay home

and make up mysteries, as we did that winter
the rain kept changing to snow and back again.
A criminal, or at least criminality

was headed right at us, just as our breaths
melted in moonlight—most like sips of syrup
a few thicker. None sinful, none unloved.

Averaged Totals

We were ready to go to war on this one.
What went around was coming around again
boring through the butch air of June
like stern notes from a viola. Plus it was plain

wrong, what those guys did. We sang
for our supper and cursed the paupers
who defaulted on their debts
passing themselves off as influencers.

Does it seem like you don't have to be
crazy to work here, but it helps?
Does it seem like the nights are getting longer?
We've slept rotten. We've disputed our fees

and our pillows are dry. Above the avenues
sleek creditors alight to preen and nidify.

An Ambulance Down in the Valley

Let’s scrape away as much as we can
before the others arrive. Though I suppose
if they bring energy drinks we’ll be fine.

Alice and them wanted fresh pajamas
for the party and as such the whole team
had to slow things way down and put

a name to, or remember the German
word for, the feeling of being happy
to be lost. We began with a sales strategy

centered on wasting everyone’s time
and honestly? To the moon. Felt great.
Political friends aired sundry ideas.

I don't understand. Where is the love? I'm
just as disgusting as everyone else.
Daily meetings might seem like a drag

until the danger passes, but every penny
I put into this risks buying high
on a boner-killing whimper. Scale back on

atoms of dope in these headwinds? No thanks.
Sorry to talk about the weather, only
snow was blowing around. The top answers

accrue through boredom, eating toast
with the brainiacs, and yes, preclusion.
I'm good if you are, or even if you'll try.

Fragment Found in a Ballot Box

Are we making progress as a community?
Answers may differ, but to call the river
impassable is a cop out, when I'm right here
in front of you with a canoe. Impassive

maybe. That I can see. You cooled on set
when your lines were dull, and we agreed
with a glance we'd suture the days shut
going forward. Peonies stunk of honey

in the dusk. I built a yurt in the yard
so we'd have a dry place to think. Hold still
a minute, you said, which killed me.
If being alone out in the open haunts

you like it does me, let me recommend
an afternoon sketching a pile of fresh laundry—

dirty works too—and then looking for solace

in someone else's sketch of something else.

Don't Just Do Something, Stand There

We felt a calm descend upon
the discussion board then, as if an ancient lion

had finally gotten the idea
of abundance through her thick skull.

It may be time to wean yourself
from velvet and give a hank of canvas

a chance. Your gift for signals
brought you this far, and if followers

prowl around under the eaves
while absolutely no one talks about you

consider it a harmless kink, since they never
really touched us, not like those tracts

adrift in the baptismal font did.
I was hunting down antique vibes

for the first time. A Roman mosaic revealed
while renovating a pizza place

or—you get the idea. I tried my best
to make the sadness strange. You could

have been mean about it, so thanks
for jumping in. A dollar for a sleeping beggar.

Pulling a curtain closed. Assurances
piled up like quilts in a basement, or a vintage

beer can collection in a different basement.

Why were you someone who slept

and awoke, and why are you now?

Sundowner

It's less a matter of courage or identifying the rebels
than just sitting with this picture of the desert. And you could
have said as much. You who loosened my reflection.
If "foreign" is a word we still use, let's tie it to the player
who keeps a quiet faith and sets aside three strands
for each one burned. In what sense have I arrived?
What have I been blind to? Earlier our enemies
pitched tents on yonder ridge and relished their genders.
I was over there forever, smug as an encyclopedia.
Now I'm not so sure. While we paused at the oasis
to let a storm pass, you mentioned a friend who had been
spared and learned to stand outside her history
without feeling it too much. I'm a bit shaky past that.
I'm dabbing at the wound you would expect.

Some old heads got the jump on us and we can let
that slide. A touch of deference seems called for.

My first winter in those parts taught me more friends
than you'd think will end up on a different level
while a fresh current, boring as milk, draws
your remaining resources beyond the breakwater
and out to sea. Any other ideas, besides that one?
Any that you can remember, I mean? Each of us
should bear our share of the burden, an eyelash trapped
in a teardrop, a white balloon's information
for a white sky. Zoom in a little and you'll see
what it means. You may even be able to hear it
from here. I paid all that extra for a window
and then fell asleep. In one ear and out the other.

Maecenas in Winter

After midnight, the river slurs its words.
I see fewer people, but they emit
more noise than ever. You're welcome

to think what you like of that. I'm not in love
with the color you chose, but I'm holding
my tongue. Remember when you asked me

to scratch our names on that HVAC unit
because all your snatched uptown friends refused
to condemn police presence on campus?

I hope we can agree I did that for you.
I hope we can agree I tucked your fiery hair
behind your ear and put my ear to yours

and listened to the liquid rush around

inside you like a nightingale. Both sides

want peace. Oh hang on, no they don't.

Reacharound

We've nailed a bunch of solid data sets
but my gut says too few. We might not doom
the throuple—don't let's go that far—

if we tack a couple years on to the sentence
already handed down, or just cop to being twice
as horny as last time and see what happens.

I totally can't tell if we're on the same page.
My former eyeballs seem stuffed with wrappers
from cans of pears, sequins and stew—occurrences—

and these fresh ones, after the computers
got in there and hawked their juice, seem persuaded
to hang back and lick pillows. What do I

need from you? Let's say a hearty supper.
You were doing everything perfect, gorgeous
in your tan pants, sometimes three times

a night, and I'm sure you never guessed referring
to my leg as "the leg"—as in, "now move the leg"—
was super helpful during the day, when a few

random kids would gather in the courtyard
to record vape trick videos. Distracting, for sure
but believing I'd die before winter, and that

it wouldn't be so hard, I built a sort of pagan
toxin under there. All our best players
sauntered off sucking their teeth. Looking

to share credentials, I suppose, or trade?

One girl kept opening the same "buy now" link in new tabs

until she must have had twenty identical carts.

Ceteris Paribus

With little hope of sleep, but no talent
for vigilance, I slid ever closer
to the edge of what our elders were pleased
to call "candy mind," where assumptions

flatten out into a kind of perfect
generosity. Night stuck blue stickers
on the schoolhouse door. Servants
taught most of the lessons, candlelight

and needlecraft chief among them.
My delayed acceptance of the peace wasn't
very inspired—you could hear that
in my voice I think, in the village song I sang

for the elders and their angels. I've got
a lot of ground to cover. The anger

either makes itself scarce or rears up right
here in front of everybody. So long

as the ancient bridge still stretches across
the bay, permitting commerce east to west
on even-numbered days and west to east
on odd—and there's no reason to believe

that will change—then all our dire schemes, all
the pros and cons we've batted back and forth
in sultry basements can't amount to anything
more authentic than a cheap mystery

splayed in the sun on a diplomat's chaise.
I can't or won't recall my Habermas.
My legs gave way—"Fear the man who fears not
to kneel"—and I glowed there on stage

until the curtain fell. I sure have seen
a lot of faces. Mail from sailors still gets through
but that's not the only factor, I know.
The redeveloped areas have brought in ringers

so attentive, so skilled in denial
of service, our monopolies seem certain
to wither in wet circles. The children
haven't understood their dreams since May

and the elders pine for less. I myself misplaced
an entire icicle in the sunrise.
The accident did in fact have significance
in that we had both eyes and bread.

The Helmet of Mambrino

It takes courage to let a thing go. Bravery
for example. Joking around is also a good one.
Who's this that struts across the plain? All alone
and hardly noble, but he's got a shine on him.
We started out early, with improvements
in mind. You picked an apple—not that kind—
and I picked an orange. The future looked
identical to a past long forgotten
by everyone save the aunties. Such stillness
on the dusty campo, as opposed to the jerks
in marketing, gone bananas for likes
as quarter-end drew nigh. Were you ever
an infant at night? I lost myself in it, I guess.
Most plans like that end in the desert.
When you spy an empty plinth, put some kids on it.
Or half again as many, if I heard you right.
The afternoon where your real mind gave way

to the other one ought brace itself for storms.

We didn't get loose by thinking things over.

We had a pot to piss in. We had a few laughs.

We built a joyful body in the tall wet grass.

Beer Money

In the past you may have heard me mention
an inalienable right of return. I'm told now
we're not quite there. My former (ish) life coach
held my gaze under a quilt while her kid
tipped water back and forth between two cups.
Don't need me. Or accuse me. And quit
clicking around in hopes erstwhile contacts
emerge from between the birches with those
"mood swatches" you ordered. It's a pamphlet
afternoon. Grackles strut in a puddle.

*

The pessimists are in our faces first
thing every weekday morning, pointing out
the obvious. We got a postcard from Stevie
and we rolled our eyes because only frigging

Stevie, who by the way never should have
married that guy in the first place, would send
a frigging postcard, like a milkmaid in a book.
Swell. The law is fine. I hope this vibe reads
as valid to you because besides this vibe
I got nada. The grease smeared on the lens
is a feature, not a bug. Good ones never stay.

*

If the songs were all exciting in the same way
that would be dull, don't you think? I'm trying
to make this even easier than it already is
which is saying something to tell the truth.
We swallow every novelty they throw at us
and belt out the same hoary saws. The future
stiffens like paste in a pot. Of everything

you've left behind, what do you miss most
is a question I'd never ask. If the blank page
seems to mock you, concentrate on a pond.

*

A knoll. An arroyo. A mea culpa in the form
of a last-second absence. Concrete steps
to muster the grit to do less. Katie bemoaned
her awful luck at the tomato competition
and we're like, what did she expect? Let go.
You've seen the movie where freckled pioneers
jolt along the rutted track, calico
buttery and hot in the sun, the clank of tack
and harness. Let go of that too. Every
now and then I'm sure to disappoint you
and that's when I'm most kissable.

Patriarchal

The dude down the block has apparently
purchased a bugle. All we held dear
has dried up like a creek in August. And we're told
kids should be taught to take a joke.

What are you going to do about it?
Conduct a traditional ceremony
complete with animals roasted in the earth
and mysterious songs?

Early adopters use up all the oxygen.
One summer they forgot to brand the cattle
but no biggie because everyone knew
exactly to whom them cattle belonged.

Penultimate Round of Approvals

Is it chilly in here for you? I mean that
plainly. I'm asking the simple questions

up front, like an average person.
My team tells me I'm a rank amateur.

With a certain flair, for sure! But don't get it twisted
at the end of the day still

a total noob, one thousand percent.
I described the song of a mockingbird

in the magnolia as a meditation
on the nature of change, and down

in Mexico the earth literally farted fire.
Do you see what I'm dealing with?

The coastal elites feel smooth
as aluminum. You say you feel seen. I'd call it

a disposable ethic, but I'm that guy who orders
salad in the city despite the risks. Poverty

comes up a lot more often lately
have you noticed that, or is it just me?

As the alarm began to sound, it drew
a margin of expertise around those

who had remained "in the boat," and we
found it a relief to consider our history

a shuttered casino haunted
by showgirl tears. To prove to us

you're human please either fail

at some point to survive disaster or

click each square containing a cloud.

Fully Deductible

We absolutely blew it by turning a blind eye
to the support we received, difficulty never
more of an urbane comedown than in this era
of self-doubt—as well as the regular kind.
A loose translation relaxes into its rhythm
like a princess smoothing her pigtails after supper.
They came to make judgments, but it wasn't
personal, and whether the floods come tomorrow
or never at all, a few misdemeanors here
and there sounds about right. You're invested
in connecting the dots to reveal a lucid
and approachable, if false, bunny. I get that.
I've plotted plenty of tricks for our time
on the high seas and tomorrow's looking
fixable. My tennis partner says he's got a guy.

Like a Lichen on the Rock

Until the beta test team had a chance

to run us through the who-what-why-where-when

we couldn't know what the gods might want with us.

Meantime the air glowed unbearably

pink and sweet, and I prayed when we got

a little older we'd learn to enjoy

the presentiments and cinnamony odors

lurking in our jeans. Most of us have kept

two sets of books. Just a few have proven

capable of genuine cruelty, losing

the selves we are required to be, but equally

losing the selves we might prefer to be.

A wave will harden into words. I'll decline

a tour of the kennels. No stomach for it.

*

A critic suggested dirt, or dirtiness, could be
a lens, which sort of makes sense? When a fault
smokes and phone poles tilt every direction
but heaven, we at least know what not
to do: keep quiet in public, confess at home. If only
everything were a book! A reflection
that shows you a stranger. Here's a house
with windows and beds and a spice rack
and here's a song written in the sand that blasts
all that to pieces. You've got to laugh.
The alert police officers who see exactly to
what you are up will laugh too, inshallah.
If you start a story already knowing
how it will end, you'll not only inconvenience
the participants, you'll out yourself as
the type with one foot in the jungle and one

that isn't even there anymore. Early navigators
always took care to learn a bit of the local patois.

*

I do this and I do that. I debouche upon the pampas
of the empty page. While the wealthy linger
in the corridor, the sunrise I'd aimed to debase
floats toward heaven shiny as a birthday balloon.
(A shout from the hammock out back: "Total war!")
And yes, sure, we could yield. We could
cede the waterways, put our feet up, close
the offices in Geneva and Dubai, permit the toner
to clot in its cartridge. But someone must write
this lemon's bitter tale. And someone is an orchard.

On Permanent Loan

I doubt our old friends would object if the emotions
the artist poured into this turbulent seascape found their way
to a much wider audience. Keep your own counsel
is solid advice. As is take seriously the plight of the monarch butterfly.

We'd best confine our passions to the safety of the freeport.
A small but thoughtfully curated selection of embarrassments
gleams on a tray beside the espresso machine. It almost feels like
my best friend got the job and didn't tell me. I paid for trash.

Though perhaps rituals of valuation are themselves ornamental?
If I may say that? My stepbrother, a total amateur, leases a shack
in a pretty stand of sassafras and does just fine. Be assured
girls all over the world tarry at open windows hoping someone

superficial will be cruel. It was never the plan. Our rivals
indulge in normal pleasures while we sit there and take it.

Phony Assignment

Could you spit it out? To settle for a warmth
wedged among the pines after all our princelings
weigh in—Well, we don't see eye to eye.
There are limits. Whether that's a comfort
or cause for an epic shit fit in the taxi
is TBD I guess. We learned internet dances

and my sister fell apart. Seemed reasonable.
Despite the boom in county revenues
water stayed wet and my heart closed its door.
Why, when the do-nothings refuse even
to acknowledge air above islands, why
would you head west without your kith and kin?

Movie Night

Shapes of light and shadow traffic the forest floor.
Can you say who starred in that? A sad one
but that it continues, and even ruins our sleep
makes us glad. Too soon after her mother dies
the churlish daughter asks for the gray kimono.
The future changes from vapor to stone
as it flows through us. Or past us. Secretly
I'm sick of guarding my privacy and would give it
to anyone willing to sneak into my house
at night and show interest in my viewing history.
On my own I struggle to believe it's real.

Now we have that one month a year the mountains
release wildflowers as evidence
new beginnings remain—box-office-wise—
solid options. We too profess our sincerity.
As the sunrise reaches its conclusion

a purple wilderness recedes. It’s no trick. Some
are determined to represent demons
in the shrubbery, some to pick figs. Why not
hole up here for a while, one-on-one.
I won’t ask about your adjectives, and since
I can’t be sure what really matters to you,
let’s agree the scene where the better daughter
misses the last train is a symbol of.

L'esprit de l'escalier

Here's where we'll perish. Our modest whistles
and kettledrums rub lotion on a bruise.

Before his success, no one ever wondered
how he got so good at pulling apart

the other stuff that was here from before.
A person can't be forced to sleep. Our friend

Cornelius was always clear on this.
"Do not teach the students to dance, reveal

to them they are already dancing." A crash
into the blackberries brings both blood

and fruit. Imagine a weak falcon takes
refuge from the rain in a privet

as you're told the library closes soon.

No one's likely to fly tonight. Happy

and serious aren't opposites, damn it.

Overruled

We're looking forward to tomorrow's matinee
with a confidence unusual for us. Quick
to grab what we can and hold onto it this time.
Those belowdecks seem unaffected.

Hardly any movement or intention follows me
down the line. My college Spanish professor
recognized me in the café and a paltry blossom
furled out, hoping for more of the same.

We spent the initial planning phases
picking at shrimp cocktail and starting
arguments no one could ever win
out there in the sand. I feel like I'm not

being transparent. The weaker centers
won't reject decay, or take a deep breath

without warning, or even send a scout
over the horizon to accept us as we are.

I know we promised no dreams, but I dreamed
my joy had a purpose, and when I brought you
your coffee and cake you said here at last
is the only mystery worth solving.

The Kuleshov Effect

Just that once, when a barroom impatience
got the better of us, we set the nudes
beside a violin and drew conclusions.
Most stones were formerly liquid, and fire's a type
of air, much like you and me. Not the best
timing but doors did open for us that summer.
I'd forgotten how real the village could be.
My lips had the gritty texture of a future truth
and I ran back along the pier in hopes
someone swimming would see it my way.

We were told it doesn't matter what time night
falls on the equator, the doves will settle.
Now I can admit how simple I am. Colleagues
and strangers alike rightly ignore
my advice and think things through on their own
lookout, welcoming a pause, less shout

and more song. All while my affection
for the juxtaposed, lately so pure, drifts off
above the glistening desert sands
as if judgment were just an extra tax to pay.

So many times, mottled by sunset pinks
in the parking lot, you showed me first one
sketch and then another. Will the skeptics
and detectives succumb to clarity, or shall
the stock methods endure? I'm glad you ask.
Stillness is a hearty milk—come in
and have a look. Some brambles beside
a book, some books beside your bed.
I've tried to dry out the supplies soaked
by the storm, but I can't vouch for them.

For You

Thanks for coming clean. Let's return to our
original strategy. Weekdays, pancakes
and a long walk along the property line
to the stand of cedar and back.

Nothing darkens, nothing is encouraged.
I'm older. You're sort of a landscape with flowers
in the foreground. When I have a question

I raise my hand and wait to be called upon.
The question I have in mind is like this evening
insofar as I've chosen it for you.

Busy Weekend

Is there any actionable difference between the exacting schemes
we reviewed last night over spinach dip and just a rough
sort of shrug to keep your shit together and act like
you been there before? Nope. Plan A is sidestep ghosts. Plan B
who knows. Maybe imagine an umbrella as you expand. Maybe
take it easy if you hear beeping behind you. I invited all my cousins
knowing full well they'd make a mess, which in my opinion
we need to normalize, like agony. As we bounced along
in the proverbial oxcart, our horny clinician rubbed quartz, sucked
the valley dry, spun on his heels, and licked his lips in a mirror.
It's a lot of action. Let's not be babies about it. We left town
because we had to, as cloud shadows wandered the meadow
like soft inedible cows. I asked you to wait outside, under
the sweetgum, where it's a bit cooler, and grab a few
more morsels wholesale, and I think that's fair, don't you?
Our story is like those stories of lost dogs turning up hungry

as a horse on the doorstep of the family's new house in Oregon.

Everything going right for once, but in the wrong way.

Staying Home to Listen to Music

No question they're aboveboard ethics-wise
but come to find out not a symbolic language.
So I was wrong, though I didn't think so.
I had nothing to say for myself, and keeping
track of downtime started to feel better
and slow, like a cousin's pet iguana stretched out
sultry under its pink bulb, not giving
one hot damn which song was next in the queue.

Out on the balcony, we did hear a few
low organ notes which seemed authentic to us.
Their desire partially brought into being
by the new possibilities of supply.
Hits keep coming from the mind of Medusa
and her crew while the rest of us stay home
to listen to music. Way I see it
I'm creating space for a few basic thrills

along the icy trenches. You wouldn't
be the first to talk up a pack of demons
lounging around on silk divans, hassling
old banjos, rapt in the immediate
caprice of the kill switch. It's a hard period.

Innovation is a weakness, which isn't good
news, it's great news. All our best employees
had that knack and sang the same tune.

El último

A sugary arm of marble beckons
from the floodlit portico. Half-human
half-star. The fashion police have canceled
most of our postures, but I have
workarounds to eyeball when you have time.
The saxophone shunned by the orchestra—
c'est moi! I sulk on my stump, munching sardines
and humming a bolero. You'll leave me much
as you found me, oblivious to the way
a day or decade can be crimped shut like
a sack of black cherries and carried home
to shine. I said what I said, then forgot it.
Something lifelike, I hope. At canasta Billy
described the San Casciano dei Bagni bronzes
and for a moment death felt abstract.
Suspended just above the canvas but not
a major figure in the scene. If a future

where we relinquished all our power dawned
on us then, and the familiar sting
was shown to be no less durable than the joy
we'd plucked from the mouths of those
who came before us, would our betters
sit still while every last luminous fragment
of finger, toe, and nose was auctioned off
as scrap? I reckon not a few have wondered.
I could nurse a grudge but I won't. It's like
you always said: "Join the club." Clear night
of many satellites. There's ours right there.

Acknowledgments & Notes

My thanks to the editors of the journals where some of these poems first appeared: *Action, Spectacle*; *Barrow Street*; *Bennington Review*; *Cherub*; *Copper Nickel*; *The Glacier*; *Michigan Quarterly Review*; *On the Seawall*; *Sixth Finch*; *Sprung Formal*; *TriQuarterly*; *Western Humanities Review*.

*

"1000 Hours of Staring" is the title of an artwork by Tom Friedman. I borrowed "mutton-headed mugwump" from Boris Johnson, of all people.

"An Onset of Palsy" is for Harold Weber.

"Beer Money" is for Fred Whiting.

"For You" is for Wendy Rawlings.

"L'esprit de l'escalier" is for Cornelius Carter.

"Like a Lichen on the Rock" is for Heather White.

"Movie Night" is for Shrode Hargis, Scott McWaters, and John Wingard.

"No Big Mystery" quotes Andre Breton: "On n'en finira jamais avec la sensation." ("We'll never be finished with sensation.")

"Staying Home to Listen to Music" is for Deanna Kreisel.

"Wrapped in Black and Yellow" is for Scott MacKenzie.

*

Thanks to Shrode Hargis, Olena Kalytiak-Davis, Deanna Kreisel, Cate Marvin, Scott McWaters, Wendy Rawlings, Matthew Rohrer, Benjamin Voigt, and Heather White for their encouragement and counsel. I am profoundly grateful to everyone at Four Way Books, the best poetry press in the universe. Thanks to Luke Dowd for letting us use his magnificent painting on the cover. My deepest thanks to my students at the University of Alabama for their constant inspiration. And to you, reader, for the gift of your attention.

About the Author

Joel Brouwer is the author of four earlier collections of poems: *Exactly What Happened*, *Centuries*, *And So*, and *Off Message*. He lives in Tuscaloosa and New Orleans and teaches at the University of Alabama.

Four Way Books is grateful to those individuals who participated in our Build a Book Program. They are:

Anonymous (10), Robert Abrams, Debra Allbery, Maggie Anderson, Kathy Aponick, Sally Ball, Jean Ball, Victor Basta, Adria Bernardi, Richard Blanchard, Laurel Blossom, adam b. bohannon, Lee Briccetti, Anthony Cappo, Anne Babson Carter, Cyrus Cassells, Jennifer Christman, Peter Coyote, Kwame Dawes, Michael Anna de Armas, Brian Komei Dempster, Patrick Donnelly, Lynn Emanuel, Joan Frank, Rigoberto González, Rachel Eliza Griffiths, Catherine Grossman, Naomi Guttman and Jonathan Mead, Beth Harrison, Jeffrey Harrison, KT Herr, Carlie Hoffman, Melissa Hotchkiss, Thomas and Autumn Howard, Parker Howe Foundation, Catherine Hoyser, Linda Susan Jackson, Elizabeth Jackson, Liz Janik, Marilyn Johnson, Deborah and Maria Jonas-Walsh, Elizabeth J. Kandall, Maeve Kinkead, Lindsay and John Landes, David Lee and Jamila Trindle, Rodney Terich Leonard, Howard Levy, Owen Lewis and Susan Ennis, Ralph and Mary Ann Lowen, Maja Lukic, Ricardo Alberto Maldonado, Donna Masini, Cleopatra Mathis, Lupe Mendez, Dale Neal, Mary Jane Nealon, Kathy Nelson, Marilyn Nelson, Nicole Nevadunsky, Kimberly Nunes, Rebecca and Daniel Okrent, Cathy McArthur Palermo, Marcia Pelletiere, Megan Pinto, Martha Rhodes, Paula Rhodes, Laurie Rosenblatt, Lyris Schonholz, Soraya Shalforoosh, Jennifer Skeele, Mary Slechta, Page Hill Starzinger, Sarah Stone, Yerra Sugarman, Marjorie and Lew Tesser, Reed Turchi, Maria Walsh, Martha Webster and Robert Fuentes, Calvin Wei, George Whalen Jr., Mark Wunderlich, Kathleen Zimmerman, and Carol Zoref.